CRITTER FITTERS™

Wearing a Mask Says I Love You

Critter Fitter Publishing
978-0-578-70472-2
Jenny Football, LLC
1950 Compass Cove Dr.
Vero Beach, FL 32963

www.getcritterfitter.com

CRITTER FITTERS™

Wearing a Mask Says I Love You

Authored by Dr. Jen Welter

Illustrated by Brooke Foley

A Jenny Football Production, Publisher

Dedicated to Nurse Jilly Bean and all the front line workers. Love to all those dedicated to protecting everyone.

Special shout out to Governor Cuomo for giving us inspiration in his daily briefings. Special thanks to Amanda Matthews.
We are stronger together, we are the inf-ANT-ry.

When bugs wake up, just like you,
bugs get up with bug things to do.
Lady Bug was looking out the window,
she wanted to get out and go.

But there was a virus no one could see,
it was the invisible enemy.
The virus hopped from bug to bug very quick,
and bugs could pass it without even feeling sick.

The bugs were told not to go out.
The virus needed carriers to move about.

Yes, viruses are very scary,
but to be passed, they must be carried.

Just like mail can only be delivered by a snail,
if no one spreads it, then the virus will fail.

The virus doesn't have its own feet,
so it can't just walk down the street!

The virus is sneaky and clingy.

It wants to come in. It is very pesky.

"I want to sneak on your hands and clothes.

Take me in through your mouth or nose."

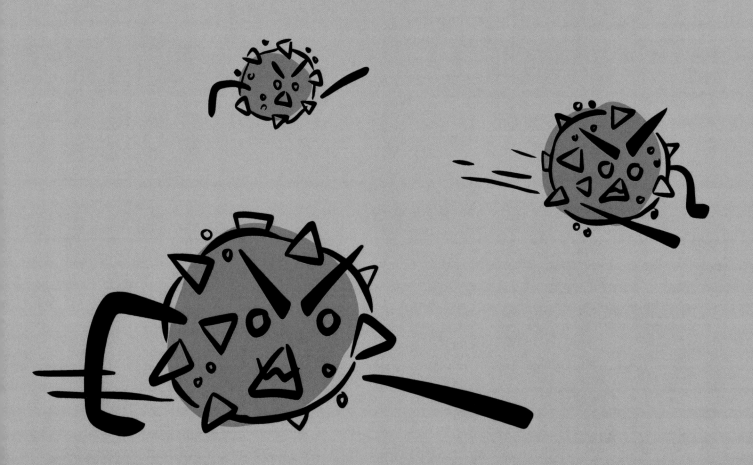

Critters don't want to become carriers,
so they wear masks as barriers.

Critters also wash their hands, wings, and all bug things.
Soap and viruses don't get along, soap shows the virus it doesn't belong.

Seeing a critter in a mask isn't cause for alarm.

A critter in a mask is trying to protect you from harm.

"When I wear a mask I protect you and me, from the virus that we can't see."

To stop the virus, the bugs stayed inside.
The bugs fought by staying home with pride.

It was as if the world was put on pause,
but all the bugs knew it was for a good cause.

Most of the bugs moving about on the streets, were working towards the virus's defeat.

The bees didn't leave their honeycomb.

The fireflies flashed their lights from home.

The spider stayed put in her web.

But, the ants chose to leave their beds.

The ANT Army was the front line of the fight.
The ANTs are soldiers who do what's right.

All bugs greeted the army with applause,
but, they wanted to do more to help the cause.

As the ANTs marched by,
Lady Bug sighed,

"Those ants are such brave bugs,
I wish I could give them hugs."

But she couldn't, and it hurt her heart,
because the world had to stay s i x f e e t a p a r t .

Lady Bug wanted to help while still staying home.

So, Lady Bug called all her bug friends on the phone.

All the bugs had ideas of what they could do.

Bugs like to help, just like you!

The ideas all came from within,
Bizzy was the first to jump in.

"I can switch from honey to delivery.
Plus, everyone can work out with me."

Then Spider said,
*"I will stop spinning webs,
and start sewing masks instead."*

"And we will give you light to work by," offered the fireflies.

Last but not least came Lady Bug,

"I'm in charge of social distance hugs!"

Over the phone, the bugs didn't feel so alone,
even though they were in their own homes.

They were connected through the heart,
even when they were far apart.

Spider worked all through the night,
thanks to the beautiful firefly light.
With the fireflies flying six feet apart and six feet above,
Spider used all eight legs to sew fast and with love.

Even masks couldn't keep their smiles hidden,
because the work felt good from deep within!

Spider handed the masks off to Bizzy.

Bizzy spread the masks by touchless delivery.

Bizzy buzzed masks to all bugs, on the ground and up above,

because all bugs can wear masks to show love.

When the ANT Army marched home that night,
they were guided by firefly light.

Bizzy needed their help for the last delivery, because Bizzy had masks for the whole ANT Army.

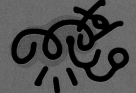

The masks fluttered down from the sky,
by the twinkling light from the fireflies.
As soon as the masks appeared,
all of the bugs clapped and cheered.

The ANTs were literally being showered with hugs,
even when they couldn't touch any other bugs.

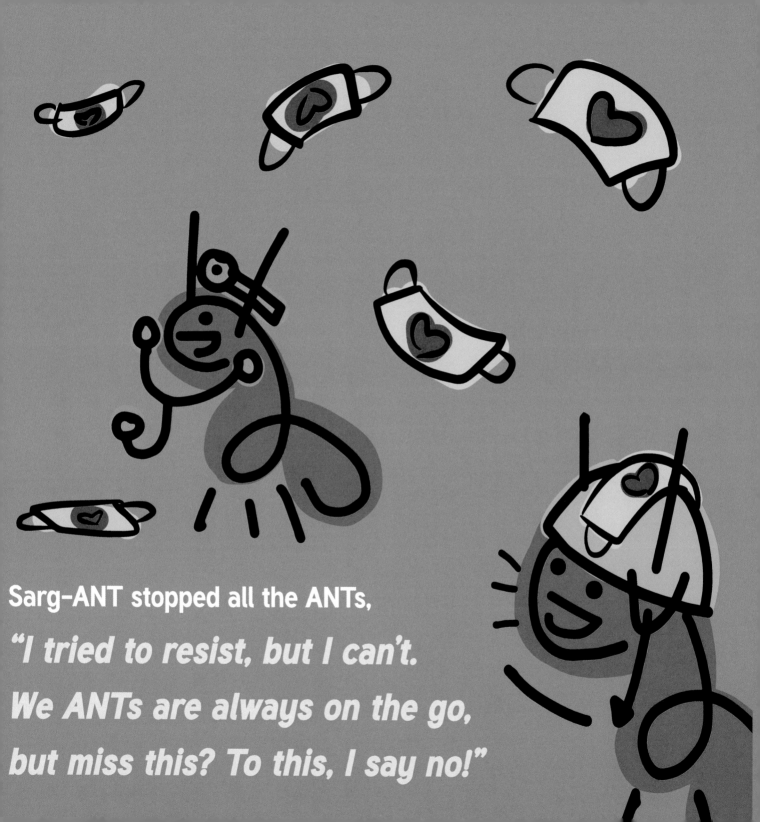

Sarg-ANT stopped all the ANTs,

"I tried to resist, but I can't.
We ANTs are always on the go,
but miss this? To this, I say no!"

Sarg-ANT looked around, assessed the scene.

Every bug had at least six feet in between.

And though wearing masks, he could feel the smiles.

They were the most loving smiles he had felt in a while.

Now with masks for every bug,
all bugs joined the ANT Army with love.

Sarg-ANT raised his arm, the bugs all went silent.

"Thank you all for doing what's right.

Thank you all for helping us fight.

Thank you for fighting the virus from your home.

We are fighting together, even when alone.

We are fighting by staying six feet apart.

Seeing you in masks warms my heart.

Wearing a mask is the right thing to do.
Wearing a mask says I Love You."

"Now little critters, put your mask on with me.
Be a part of the ANT Army!